THE FLEURY PLAY OF HEROD

THE FLEURY PLAY
OF HEROD

EDITED BY

TERENCE BAILEY

TORONTO

PONTIFICAL INSTITUTE OF MEDIAEVAL STUDIES

1965

Printed in The Netherlands by Royal VanGorcum Ltd., Assen

TABLE OF CONTENTS

uos scribe interrogam dierat si qd de hõ puero septem ude
te scibe dni reuoluat libru
grandi iuentia est ppheciat
diceat. Quidam die nostri
res cum digito. Regi uere
rim̄ in libro.   dulo tdant librum.   Quidm die ipphiau

linea natei xpo in betleem ude euntante daind ppha sic
te herodes uns
propheciat ture ꝯ
neceſſ picat libro
at fili eius quatro us
multu. poestat par
uancinaut   erbleem no est minima.   sicatuiuf paret uis
luti et eu

Solue pater melior. salue rex egregie. quid ubiq̄ imper

ceptra tenet regia. Ouli amantiſſime digne laudis munere

laudis pōpa regie tuo geuens nonnue. Rex est natus sorcior
et silua
desper h
x. oste
et ead un
uield de

nobis et potencior. ueueor ne solio uos excubet regis.

sont illei regulu. qr natu paruulum iube pax sibi̇ n
te domum dimittat herodes
magos ut inqrate de puero
ꝯcorn eis ſpondeat regi
mire preliu nato dicens.

INTRODUCTION

Medieval dramatizations of the events surrounding Christ's birth are preserved in the manuscripts of many churches from northern Europe to Sicily. The plays vary widely in the extent of their treatment of the theme, but almost without exception they are closely related, and share much of the same material. Not all of these works have survived intact. In some cases there are irreparable lacunae. More often the music is preserved in a notation too primitive to reveal more than vague outlines.

Of the works whose text and music can be recovered, the present one is the most interesting. For one thing, it is the most extensive version. In fact, it contains most of the traditional dialogue common to this family of Christmas plays, and on this ground is their best representative. Moreover, this traditional material is sewn together with a dramatic skill not to be taken for granted in such early efforts. The rubrics are not extensive, but are enough to provide clear indications of the action.

The book which contains the play, now MS 201 in the municipal library of Orléans, was written about the year 1200, and used at the monastery of Saint-Benoît-sur-Loire in Fleury. But as clues to the date and provenance of the work these facts must be considered in the light of what was said above. Most of the text was already widely known in the eleventh century. What may be attributed to the author of the Fleury play is the present form of the work: the scope of the action, the order of the scenes, some additional dialogue, and certain touches in the wording.

The primary sources for the events of the drama are the narratives of the evangelists Matthew and Luke. But to supplement these sparse accounts there has been recourse to the apocryphal Infancy Gospels. Works like the *History of the Infant Saviour*, the so-called *Proto-Gospel of St. James*, and the *Pseudo-Gospel of St. Matthew*, which claim to relate in detail the circumstances of the Nativity, were widely known at a very early date. Their legends were popular subjects for poets and artists in the middle ages.

The text of the play demonstrates the medieval predilection for centonism. The Angel's announcement and the two following utterances of the Shepherds are taken from Luke, II, 10-15. The dialogue between the Shepherds and the Midwives is adapted from a trope to the introit of the third Mass of Christmas Day. The Shepherds' invitation to the audience to worship the Christ Child and the processional sung by the Magi as they approach Jerusalem are taken from antiphons for the Feast of Epiphany. The prophecy found by Herod's Scribes (and sung by the Chorus) is an antiphon for the second Sunday of Advent. The piece sung by the Shepherds returning from the manger and their dialogue with the Magi are taken from responds for the Feast of Christmas. The processional sung by the Magi on the way to the manger is an Epiphany sequence. The Magi's recessional is an antiphon for the Christmas Octave. Very interesting is a reference to Virgil. The Armed Man's first speech is after the *Aeneid*, VIII., 112-114.

It should be said to the merit of the play that this borrowing was not done slavishly. The gleaned material is often modified to make it appropriate. To give just one example of this, the words of the Epiphany sequence, 'haec *magorum* occulos' ('this the *wise men's* eyes'), become in the mouths of the Magi, 'haec *nostrorum* occulos' ('this *our* eyes').

In the case of textual borrowings from the liturgy the music too was taken over. This accounts for certain inconsistencies in the style. For example, the rather ornate setting of the simple

phrase, 'quem vidistis?' ('whom did you see?'), is that of the
Christmas respond which begins with these same words. It is
interesting to note that the music for the latter part of the
Angel's announcement and that of the Shepherds' reply to
the Magi are taken from different versions of the same respond.

Because the play is composed of diverse elements – even
the original contributions, it will be remembered, are from
different pens and different centuries – it presents a number of
distinct literary and musical styles. The borrowed lines, except
those taken from the sequence and, of course, those from the
Aeneid, are prose. The poetry, which includes most of the
original dialogue, is partly based on classical models which
feature quantitative accent, and partly in the more modern
style featuring stress accents and rhyme.

The music is mostly of a moderate character, employing
neither long melismas nor a great compass. In contrast is the
more assuming cantilena of the trope and the responds, and
the severely syllabic setting of the sequence. One of the well-
known features of plainsong is the frequent appearance of
certain short musical phrases, especially opening and closing
figures. But in this play, musical repetition has been used above
this, unmistakably to underline the correspondence between
certain speeches. The rhythm, as indicated in the manuscript
by the customary thirteenth-century chant notation of the
region around Fleury, is the unmeasured, oratorical rhythm of
plainsong. A striking exception will be found in the dialogue
between Herod and his son. In this case the poetic metre
employed for the scene – evidently one of the most recent
additions to the play – suggested a transcription in keeping
with the newer metrical music coming into prominence in
France about the time of the Fleury manuscript.

The directions supplied for the present play are meagre, as
they are for most of the medieval dramas. But enough infor-

mation survives in one place or another to permit some generalizations. First of all, it will be clear from the rubrics of the present play alone that a life-like representation was intended. We are not here concerned, as it were, with oratorio. Elaborate stage properties and machinery were known. For example at Moosburg, near Munich, at the climax of a representation of the Resurrection, an effigy of Christ, with flowers, a dove, and an angel, was raised from the floor by means of ropes to disappear through an opening in the roof. But such laboriously contrived effects were rare. For the most part the staging was suggested with the existing fixtures and features of the church. The altar – the repository of the consecrated Host – was by patristic tradition both the mystical cradle and sepulchre of Christ, and frequently represented them in the Christmas and Easter dramas. For the more ordinary requirements of the plays, benches and tables, thrones, doorways, steps, crypts, and elevated walkways were in every large church readily available. The use of the building itself for the setting had certain advantages. The grandeur of a large cathedral or conventual church allowed a freedom of action not possible in the largest of modern theatres. Many of the plays call for processions, and these, for example, are far more effective in church aisles than on stage.

Costumes were most often improvised from sacristy vestments arranged and combined for the purpose in unusual ways, and supplemented with such distinctive insignia as crowns, sceptres, swords, and shepherds' crooks. But not all the costumes were clerical. Rubrics will specify that certain participants are to be dressed in the clothing of youths, of young girls, or of women. Only very rarely are costumes described in more detail.

Make-up was not unknown. It was customary in the Christmas plays for one of the Magi to have his face blackened.

[12]

And although monks and clerks were clean-shaven, they were required, on occasion, to impersonate bearded men.

It is clear that the women's roles in the plays were normally taken by men or boys – a custom familiar to us as late as the seventeenth century in the plays of Shakespeare. It should be said, though, that productions with both men and women were not impossible in the middle ages. Accounts survive of plays at convents of women in England, at Barking, and in France, at Troyes, where some of the parts were taken by nuns.

There is direct evidence for the participation of instrumental music in a play at the very end of the medieval period, a representation from the late fourteenth century of the Presentation of the Virgin Mary in the Temple. Rubrics of the earlier period are silent on this matter, but there is reason to believe that an instrumental accompaniment was customary in the church dramas. The early Christian prejudice against instruments had died out in the West at least by the seventh century. They were freely used in church in the middle ages to accompany both the liturgical chant and the new polyphony, and especially for festive occasions important enough to warrant the performance of plays. Many lines, such as these from a work performed in the twelfth century at Beauvais:

> Simul omnes gratulemur;
> Resonent et tympana;
> Cythariste tangant cordas;
> Musicorum organa
> Resonent ad eius preconia

seem almost to demand instrumental accompaniment.

The lines from Beauvais just quoted refer to drums, to a harp, or something like it with plucked strings, and to other unspecified 'instruments of music.' Some of the others which were considered suitable for sacred music can be seen in a widespread medieval drawing in which *Musica Sacra* is represented by King David the psalmist and attendant musicians. David holds, of course, a harp. In a twelfth-century version of the drawing from St. John's, Cambridge, those attending play mounted bells, monochord, flute, horn, and organ. In an eleventh-century version now at the Bibliothèque Nationale in Paris we find a fiddle and a bowed lyre.

We can only guess at what these instruments played. There can be no question of harmony in the modern sense of the word. It seems likely that the accompaniments were heterophonic, like those used for the modern monophony of China, Japan, India, and the Arab world. In this style each participant plays essentially the same melody, but ornamented or simplified according to the character of the music and the capabilities of his instrument. Complementary rhythms, drones, and even occasional chords are also possible.

It would be wrong to think that the main purpose of the medieval liturgical drama was amusement. This was part of it, of course; there are even unmistakable attempts at humour. But primarily the plays were to make vivid the events commemorated in the Office on certain great occasions. In fact, there is reason to believe that many of the works were themselves thought of as religious services. This is clear from certain features, for example in the present play, the Shepherds' invitation to the audience to join in worship of the Christ-child. This intention is evident too from the frequent title, 'office', as in 'Officium Pastorum' (the Office of the Shepherds), 'Officium Stelle' (the Office of the Star), and 'Officium Regum Trium' (the Office of the Three Kings), which is given to the works.

The earliest of the liturgical dramas seem to have been suggested by the dramatic character of certain texts occurring in the Mass and Office. These brief and ingenuous efforts were performed as interpolations scarcely interrupting the course of the liturgy. The longer and more developed dramas of the later medieval period usually retained some connection with the ordinary liturgical services. Very often they were presented at the close of matins. This was certainly the setting of the Fleury play, for a cue to the *Te Deum*, the last hymn of the morning office, occurs at the close of the dialogue. Matins is the first, the longest, and the most solemn of the seven canonical offices, and as its 'lessons' normally relate the events and explain the significance of the day's liturgy, it was an ideal time for dramatizations of the same theme.

A few words now about the manuscript and the edition. MS 201 of the Orléans Municipal Library contains some 251 pages of different sizes in several hands. The first 175 pages are devoted to sermons and other spiritual writings; the last seven to two proses, one for St. Lomer, with music, and one to the Virgin, without. Four folio gatherings contain ten liturgical dramas, written, except for corrections, by the same hand: four on miracles of St. Nicholas: The Dowried Daughters, The Three Clerks, The Image of St. Nicholas, and The Sons of Gedron; The Play of Herod, The Holy Women at Christ's Tomb, The Apparition at Emmaus, and The Resurrection of Lazarus. The present play occupies pages 205-214. In the edition, a diagonal slash indicates the end of a manuscript page.

One or two things must be said about the transcription of the neums. Following the practice of Solesmes, an eighth note has been used to represent the basic unit of the chant. All notes written together belong to one syllable. Liquescents are indicated by a short horizontal stroke drawn through the note stems.

The Latin text has been printed twice, the second time without music, in order that the literary forms may be clearly seen. The verse has been arranged in hexameters, or else to display rhyme and assonance. In order to have a clear text with the music, the footnotes which refer to the wording appear in this second part of the edition. It has not been thought necessary to include more than the manuscript's cue to the long hymn, *Te Deum*. This is available in any number of modern editions.

TEXT AND MUSIC

Incipit ordo ad representandum Herodem

Parato Herode et ceteris personis, tunc quidam Angelus cum multitudine in excelsis
appareat. Quo viso Pastores perterriti, salutem annunciet eis de ceteris adhuc tacencibus:

No - li - te ti - me - re vos, ec - ce e - nim

e - van - ge - li - zo vo - bis gau - di - um ma - gnum

quod e - rit om - ni po - pu - lo, qui - a na - tus

est vo - bis ho - di - e sal - va - tor

mun - di in ci - vi - ta - te Da - vid,

et hoc vo - bis si - gnum: in - ve - ni - e - tis

in - fan - tem pan - nis in - vo - lu - tum et

po - si - tum in pre - se - pi - o in

[19]

me – di – o du - um   a – ni – ma – li – um.

Et subito omnis multitudo cum Angelo dicat:

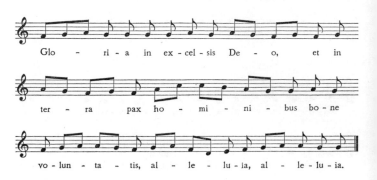

Glo –   ri - a   in ex - cel - sis De –   o,   et in

ter –   ra   pax ho –   mi –   ni –   bus bo - ne

vo - lun – ta – tis, al – le – lu – ia, al – le - lu – ia.

Tunc demum surgentes, cantent intra se *Transeamus,* et cetera, et sic procedant usque ad
presepe quod ad ianuas monasterii paratum erit:

Tran - se –   a – mus   us – que   Beth - le – hem, et

vi – de –   a –   mus   hoc   ver - bum quod fac – tum   est,

quod   fe – cit Do - mi – nus et   os – ten – dit no - bis.

Tunc due Mulieres custodientes presepe interrogent Pastores, dicentes:

Quem   que – ri – tis, Pas –
to – res, di – ci – te?

Respondeant Pastores:

Sal – va – to – rem Chris-tum Do –
mi – num, in-fan – tem pan – nis in – vo-lu – tum
se – cun-dum ser – mo – nem an – ge – li – cum.

Mulieres:

Ad – est   par – vu – lus cum Ma –
ri – a ma – tre   e – ius, de quo du – dum

*this passage reads a third higher in the MS. It is likely that the initial has covered a clef.

[21]

va - ti - ci - nan - do Y - sa - i - as pro - phe -

ta di - xe - rat: ec - ce vir - go con -

ci - pi - et et pa - ri - et fi - li - um.

Tunc Pastores, procidentes, adorent infantem, dicentes:

Sal - ve, Rex Se - cu - lo - rum!

Postea, surgentes, invitent populum circumstantem adorandum infantem, dicentes tribus vicibus:

Ve - ni - te, ve - ni - te, ve - ni - te a - do - re - mus

De - um, qui - a ip - se est Sal - va - tor nos - ter.

Interim Magi, prodeuntes quisquam de angulo suo quasi de regione sua, conveniant ante altare vel ad ortum stelle. Dum appropinquant primus dicat:

Stel - la ful - go - re ni - mi - o ru - ti - lat.

Secundus:

Que Re - gem Re - gum na - tum de - mon - strat,

Tercius:

Quem ven - tu - rum o - lim pro - phe - ta si - gna - ve - rat.

Tunc, stantes collaterales, dicat dexter ad medium, *Pax tibi, Frater,* et ille respondeat, *Pax quoque tibi,* et osculentur sese; sic medius ad sinistrum, sic sinister ad dextrum. Salutacio cuiusque:

Pax ti - bi, Fra - ter.

Responsio cuiusque:

Pax quo - que ti - bi.

Tunc ostendant stellam sibi mutuo. Primus:

Ec - ce stel - la!

Secundus:

Ec - ce stel - la!

*from Paris, Bibl. Nat. MS lat. 904, f. 28v

[23]

Tercius:

Ec - ce stel - la!

Procedente autem stella, sequantur et ipsi precedentem stellam, dicentes:

E - a - mus er - go et in - qui - ra - mus e - um,

of - fe - ren - tes e - i mu - ne - ra,

au - rum, thus, et mir - ram; qui - a

scrip - tum di - di - ci - mus: a - do - ra - bunt e - um om - nes

re - ges, om - nes gen - tes ser - vi - ent e - i.

Venientes ad hostium chori, interrogent astantes:

Di - ci - te no - bis, O Ie - ro - so - li - mi - ta -

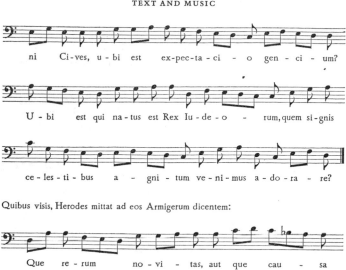

ni Ci - ves, u - bi est ex - pec - ta - ci - o gen - ci - um?

U - bi est qui na - tus est Rex Iu - de - o - rum, quem si - gnis

ce - les - ti - bus a - gni - tum ve - ni - mus a - do - ra - re?

Quibus visis, Herodes mittat ad eos Armigerum dicentem:

Que re - rum no - vi - tas, aut que cau - sa

su - be - git vos I - gno - tas tem - pta - re vi - as?

Quo ten - di - tis er - go? Quod ge - nus? Un - de

do - mo? Pa - cem - ne huc fer - tis an ar - ma?

Responsio Magorum:

Chal - de - i su - mus; Pa - cem fe - ri - mus.

[25]

Re - gem Re - gum que - ri - mus Quem na - tum es - se
stel - la in - di - cat, Que ful - go - re

ce - te - ris cla - ri - or ru - ti - lat.

Armiger, reversus, salutet Regem. Flexu genu dicat:

Vi - vat Rex in e - ter - num!

Herodes:

Sal - vet te, gra - ti - a me - a.

Armiger, ad Regem:

Ad - sunt no - bis, Do - mi - ne, tres
vi - ri i - gno - ti ab o - ri - en - te

ve - ni - en - tes, no - vi - ter na - tum

quem - dam re - gem que - ri - tan - tes.

Tunc mittat Herodes Oratores vel Interpretes ad Magos, dicens:

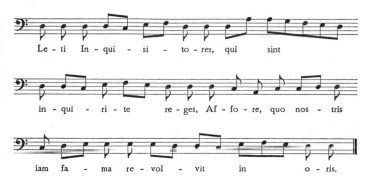

Le - ti In - qui - si - to - res, qui sint

in - qui - ri - te re - ges, Af - fo - re, quo nos - tris

iam fa - ma re - vol - vit in o - ris.

Interpretes ad Magos:

Prin - ci - pis e - dic - tu, Re - ges, pres - cri - re

ve - ni - mus Quo sit di - rec - tus

hic ves - ter et un - de pro - fec - tus.

Magi:

Re - gem que - si - tum du - ce stel - la
si - gni - fi - ca - tum, Mu - ne - re pro - vi - so
pro - pe - ra - mus e - um ve - ne - ran - do.

Oratores, reversi ad Herodem:

Re - ges sunt A - ra - bum. Cum tri - no
mu - ne - re na - tum Que - runt in - fan -
tem quem mon - strant si - de - ra re - gem.

Herodes mittens Armigerum pro magis:

An - te ve - ni - re iu - be, quo pos - sim

sin - gu - la sci - re Qui sint, cur ve - ni - ant,

quo - nam ru - mo - re re - qui-rant.

Armiger:

Quod man-das, ci - ci - us, Rex in -cli - te, pro - fi - ci - e-tur.

Armiger, ad Magos:

Re - gi - a vos man-da - ta vo-cant. Non se - gni-ter i - te!

Armiger, adducens Magos ad Herodem:

En Ma - gi ve - ni - unt, Et re - gem

na - tum, stel - la du - ce, re - qui-runt.

Herodes, ad Magos:

Que sit cau - sa vi - e? Qui

vos, vel un - de ve - ni - tis? Di - ci - te!

Magi:

Rex est cau - sa vi - e; re - ges

su - mus ex A - ra - bi - tis Huc ve - ni - en - tes.

Que - ri - mus en Re - gem re-gnan-ti - bus im - pe - ri - tan-tem,

Quem na - tum mun - do lac-tat Iu - da - i - ca vir - go.

Herodes, ad Magos:

Re - gem quem que - ri - tis,

na - tum es - se quo si - gno di - di - cis - tis?

Magi:

Il – lum na – tum es – se di – di – ci – mus in

o – ri – en – te stel – la mon – stran – te.

Herodes:

Si il – lum re – gna – re cre – di – tis, di – ci – te no – bis!

Magi:

Il – lum re – gna – re fa – ten – tes, cum mis – ti – cis

mu – ne – ri – bus de ter – ra lon – gin – qua a – do –

ra – re ve – ni – mus, ter – num De – um

ve – ne – ran – tes tri – bus cum mu – ne – ri – bus.

Et ostendant munera. Primus dicat:

Au - ro re - gem.

Secundus:

Thu - re De - um.

Tercius:

Mir - ra mor - ta - lem.

Tunc Herodes imperet Simmistis, qui cum eo sedent in habitu iuvenili, ut adducant Scribas, qui in diversorio parati sunt barbati:

Vos me - i Sim - mis - te, Le - gis pe - ri - tos as -

ci - te ut dis - cant in pro - phe - tis quid sen - ci - ant ex his.

Simmiste ad Scribas, et adducant eos cum libris prophetarum:

Vos, Le - gis pe - ri - ti, ad Re - gem vo - ca - ti, cum

pro - phe - ta - rum li - bris pro - pe - ran - do ve - ni - te!

Postea Herodes interroget Scribas, dicens:

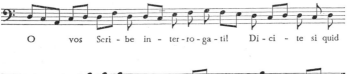

O vos Scri - be in - ter - ro - ga - ti! Di - ci - te si quid

de hoc pu - e - ro scrip - tum vi - de - ri - tis in li - bro.

Tunc Scribe diu revolvant librum, et tandem, inventa quasi prophecia, dicant *Vidimus Domine,* et ostendentes cum digito, Regi incredulo tradant librum:

Vi - di - mus, Do - mi - ne, in pro - phe - ta - rum li - ne - is,

nas ci Chris - tum in Beth - le - hem Iu - de, ci - vi - ta -

te Da - vid, pro - phe - ta sic va - ti - ci - nan - te:

Chorus!

Beth - le - hem non es mi - ni - ma in

prin - ci - pi - bus Iu - da, ex te e - nim e - xi - et

[33]

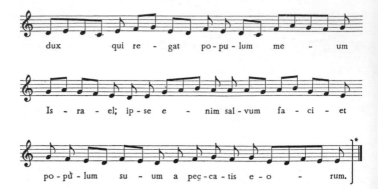

dux   qui re - gat po - pu - lum me - um

Is - ra - el; ip-se e - nim sal-vum fa - ci - et

po - pŭ - lum su - um a peç-ca - tis e - o - rum.

Tunc Herodes, visa prophecia, fuore accessus, proiciat librum. At Filius eius, audito tumultu, procedat pacificaturus patrem, et stans, salutet eum:

Sal - ve, Pa - ter in - cli - te, Sal - ve, Rex, ę - gre - gi - e

Qui u - bi - que im - pe - ras Scep - tra te - nens re - gi - a.

Herodes:

Fi - li a - man - tis - si - me, Di - gne lau - dis

mu - ne - re, Lau - dis pom - pam re - gi - e Tu - o

*from Codex F 160 of Worcester Cathedral, p. 9
*in the MS this note is repeated, probably carelessly

ge - rens no - mi - ne, Rex est na - tus for - ci - or

No - bis, et po - ten - ci - or. Ve - re - or ne

so - li - o Nos ex - tra - het re - gi - o.

Tunc Filius, despective loquens de Christo, offerat se ad vindictam, dicens:

Con - tra il - lum re - gu-lum, Con - tra na - tum par-vu-lum

Iu - be, Pa - ter, fi - li - um Hoc in - i - re pre-li - um.

Tunc demum dimittat Herodes Magos ut inquirant de puero, et coram eis spondeat Regi
nato, dicens:

I - te, et de pu - e - ro di - li - gen - ter in - ves -

ti - ga - te, Et in - ven - to, re-de-un-tes mi-chi re-nun-ci -

[35]

a - te Ut et e-go ve-ni - ens a - do - rem e - um.

Magis egredientibus, procedat stella eos, que nondum in conspectu Herodis appareat.
Quam ipsi sibi mutuo ostendentes, procedant (Qua visa, Herodes et Filius minentur cum
gladiis.):

Ec - ce stel - la · in o - ri - en - te

pre - vi - sa i - te - rum pro - ce - dit nos lu - ci - da!

Interim Pastores redeuntes a presepe veniant, gaudentes et cantantes in eundo:

O Re - gem Ce - li, cu - i ta - li -

a fa - mu - lan - tur ob - se-qui - a!

Sta-bu-lo po - ni - tur qui con -

ti - net mun - dum. Ja - cet in pre - se - pi -

o et in nu - bi - bus to - nat

*from Codex F 160 of Worcester Cathedral, p. 30

[36]

Ad quos Magi:

Quem vi – dis – tis?

Pastores:

Se - cun - dum   quod dic - tum est no - bis

ab an – ge – lo   de pu – e - ro is – to,

·in – ve – ni - mus in - fan - tem pan   nis

in - vo - lu - tum et po - si – tum in pre - se pi - o

in me - di - o du - um a – ni - ma - li – um.

Postea, Pastoribus abeuntibus, Magi procedant post stellam usque ad presepe, cantantes:

Quem non pre - va - lent pro - pri - a ma - gni - tu - di - ne

[37]

Ce - lum, ter - ra at - que ma - ri - a la - ta ca - pe - re,

De vir - gi - ne - o na - tus u - te - ro po - ni - tur

in pre - se - pi - o. Ser - mo ce - ci - nit quem va - ti -

di - cus: stant si - mul bos et a - si - nus. Sed o - ri - tur

stel - la lu - ci - da, pre - bi - tu - ra Do - mi - no

ob - se - qui - a, Quam Ba - la - am ex Iu - da - i - ca

nas - ci - tu - ram di - xe - rat pro - sa - pi - a. Hec nos - tro - rum

oc - cu - los ful - gu - ran - ti lu - mi - ne pres - trin - xit

lu - ci - da, Et nos ip - sos pro - vi - de du - cens ad

cu - na - bu - la res - plen - dens ful - gi - da.

Tunc Obstetrices, videntes Magos, alloquantur:

Qui sunt hi - i qui, stel - la du - ce,

nos a - de - un - tes i - nau - di - ta fe - runt?

Magi:

Nos su - mus, quos cer - ni - tis, re - ges Thar - sis

et A - ra - bum et Sa - ba do - na fe - ren - tes

Chris - to na - to, Re - gi, Do - mi - no, quem

[39]

stel - la du - cen - te, a - do - ra - re ve - ni - mus.

Obstetrices, ostendentes puerum:

Ec - ce pu - er a - dest quem que - ri - tis; iam

pro - pe - ra - te et a - do - ra - te, qui - a

ip - se est re - demp - ci - o mun - di.

Magi, primus:

Sal - ve, Rex se - cu - lo - rum!

Secundus:

Sal - ve, De - us de - o - rum!

Tercius:

Sal - ve, sa - lus mor - tu - o - rum!

Tunc, procidentes, Magi adorent puerum et offerent. Primus dicat:

Sus - ci - pe, Rex, au - rum, re - gis si - gnum.

Secundus:

Sus - ci - pe thus, Tu ve - re De - us.

Tercius:

Sus - ci - pe mir - ram, si - gnum se - pul - tu - re.

Istis factis, Magi incipiant dormire ibi ante presepe donec Angelus (desuper apparens) moneat in sompnis ut redeant in regionem suam per aliam viam. Angelus dicat:

Im - ple - ta sunt om - ni - a que pro - phe - ti - ce

scrip - ta sunt. I - te, vi - am re - me - an - tes a -

li - am, nec de - la - to - res tan - ti

[41]

Re - gis pu - ni - en - di e - ri - tis.

Magi, evigilantes:

De - o gra - ci - as! Sur - ga - mus er - go,

vi - si - o - ne mo - ni - ti an - ge - li - ca,

et cal - le mu - ta - to, la - te - ant He -

ro - dem que vi - di - mus de pu - e - ro.

Tunc Magi, abeuntes, cantent per aliam viam, non vidente Herode:

O ad - mi - ra - bi - le com - mer - ci - um!

Cre - a - tor ge - ne - ris hu - ma - ni a - ni - ma - tum

cor - pus su - mens, de vir - gi - ne nas - ci di -

gna - tus est. Et pro - ce - dens ho - mo

si - ne se - mi - ne, lar - gi - tus

est no - bis su - am de - i - ta - tem.

Tunc, venientes in choro dicentes:

Gau - de - te, Frat - res, Chris - tus

no - bis na - tus est, De - us ho - mo fac - tus est.

Tunc cantor incipit:

Te De - um

Sic Finit.

*from Codex F 160 of Worcester Cathedral, p. 50

[43]

LATIN TEXT AND ENGLISH TRANSLATION

[I]ncipit ordo ad representandum Herodem.

Parato Herode et ceteris personis, tunc quidam Angelus cum multitudine in excelsis ap[p]areat. Quo viso Pastores perterriti, salutem[1] annunciet eis de ceteris adhuc tacencibus:

> *Nolite timere vos, ecce[2] enim evangelizo vobis gaudium magnum quod erit omni populo, quia natus est vobis[3] [h]odie salvator mundi in civitate David, et hoc vobis signum: invenietis infantem pannis involutum et positum in presepio in medio duum animalium.*

Et subito omnis multitudo cum Angelo dicat:

> *Gloria in excelsis Deo, et in terra pax hominibus bone voluntatis, alleluia, alleluia.*

Tunc demum surgentes, cantent intra se *Transeamus*, et cetera, et sic procedant usque ad presepe quod ad ianuas monasterii paratum erit:

> *Transeamus usque Bethle[h]em, et videamus/ hoc verbum quod factum est, quod fecit Dominus et ostendit nobis.*

Tunc due Mulieres custodientes presepe interrogent Pastores, dicentes:

Quem queritis, Pastores, dicite.

---

[1] MS: salus   [2] inserted between the lines   [3] MS: nobis

Here begins the play of Herod.

When Herod and the rest of the characters are ready, let an Angel appear with a multitude on high. To the Shepherds, terrified at this sight, the Angel, from the midst of the multitude (which so far has remained silent), shall proclaim this greeting:

> *Fear not, for behold I bring you tidings of great joy for all nations. This day, for your sake, in the city of David, the saviour of the world is born. And this will be your sign: you will find a child in swaddling clothes lying between two beasts in a manger.*

And at once the whole multitude shall sing with the Angel:

> *Glory to God in the highest, and on earth peace to men of good will, alleluia, alleluia.*

The Shepherds shall then rise up, singing among themselves *Transeamus*, etc., and proceed to the manger prepared at the gates of the monastery:

> *Let us make our way to Bethlehem and look into what has been said. Let us see what the Lord has done and made known to us.*

Then the two Women watching over the manger shall question the Shepherds, singing:

> *Say, Shepherds, whom you are seeking.*

Respondeant Pastores:

> *Salvatorem Christum Dominum, infantem pannis involutum secundum sermonem angelicum.*

Mulieres:

> *Adest parvulus cum Maria matre eius, de quo dudum vaticinando Ysaias propheta dixerat: ecce virgo[1] concipiet et pariet filium.*

Tunc Pastores, procidentes, adorent infantem, dicentes:

> *Salve, Rex Seculorum!*

Postea, surgentes, invitent populum circumstantem adorandum infantem, dicentes tribus vicibus:

> *Venite, venite, venite adoremus Deum, quia ipse est Salvator noster.*

Interim Magi, prodeuntes quisquam de angulo suo quasi de regione sua, conveniant ante altare vel ad ortum stelle. Dum appropinquant primus dicat:

> *Stella fulgore nimio rutilat,|*

Secundus:

> *[Que Regem Regum natum demonstrat,][2]*

---

[1] MS: vrirgo

[2] in the MS this speech is lacking. It is supplied here from Paris, Bibliothèque Nationale, MS lat. 904 (of the thirteenth century, from Rouen), fol. 28v.

The Shepherds shall reply:

> *Christ the Lord Saviour, a child in swaddling clothes according to the Angel's tidings.*

The Women:

> *The little one is here with Mary his mother. Of this the prophet Isaiah spoke prophetically: behold a virgin will conceive and bring forth a son.*

Then the Shepherds, throwing themselves to the ground, shall worship the child, singing:

> *Blessed be the King of Ages!*

Afterwards, rising up, they shall invite those present to worship the child, singing three times:

> *Come, come, come let us worship him, our God and Saviour.*

Meanwhile the Magi, coming each from his own corner as though from his native land, shall meet before the altar at the starting-point of the star. And as they approach let the first sing:

> *Radiant as lightning shines the star,*

The second:

> *Which lights the birth of the King of Kings,*

[Tercius]¹

Quem venturum olim propheta signaverat.

Tunc, stantes collaterales, dicat dexter ad medium, *Pax tibi,*
Frater, et ille respondeat, *Pax quoque tibi*, et osculentur sese;
sic medius ad sinistrum, sic sinister ad dextrum. Salutacio
cuiusque:

Pax tibi, Frater.

Responsio³ cuiusque:

Pax quoque tibi.

Tunc ostendant [stellam] sibi mutuo⁴. [Primus dicat]⁵:

Ecce stella!

[Secundus:]

Ecce stella!

[Tercius:]

Ecce stella!

Procedente autem stella, sequantur⁶ et ipsi precedentem stellam,
dicentes:

¹ see note 2 above. In the MS these lines are given to the second *Magus*.
² the liturgical Kiss of Peace.
³ MS: respondus

The third:

Whose coming the prophet long ago foretold.

Then, standing side by side, the one on the right shall sing to the one in the middle, *Pax tibi, Frater.* And he shall reply, *Pax quoque tibi.* And they shall exchange the Kiss[2]; and similarly the one in the middle with respect to the one on the left, and he to the one on the right. The greeting of each:

Peace to you, Brother.

The reply of each:

And peace to you.

Then they shall point out the star to one another. Let the first sing:

Look, the star!

The second:

Look, the star!

The third:

Look, the star!

As the star moves off let them follow, singing, as it precedes:

[4] the last two letters are illegible, and corrected in the margin
[5] the distribution of these utterances is clear in the MS from the use of large initials　　　[6] MS: sequentur

*Eamus ergo et inquiramus eum, offerentes ei munera,
aurum, thus, et mirram; quia scriptum didicimus: ado-
rabunt eum omnes reges, omnes gentes servient ei.*

Venientes ad hostium chori, interrogent astantes:

*Dicite nobis, O Ierosolimitani Cives, ubi est expectacio
gencium? Ubi est qui natus est Rex Iudeorum, quem
signis celestibus agnitum venimus adorare?*

Quibus visis, Herodes mit[t]at ad eos Armigerum dicentem[1]:

*Que rerum| novitas, aut que causa subegit vos
Ignotas temptare vias? Quo tenditis ergo?
Quod genus? Unde domo? Pacemne huc fertis an arma?*

Responsio Magorum:

*C[h]aldei sumus;
Pacem ferimus.
Regem Regum querimus
Quem natum esse stella indicat,
Que fulgore ceteris clarior rutilat.*

Armiger, reversus, salutet[2] Regem. Flexo genu dicat:

Vivat Rex in eternum!

[1] MS: dicens
[2] MS: salutat

> Let us go, therefore, and look for him, and offer gifts
> of gold, incense, and myrrh to affirm what is written:
> all kings will worship him, and every people serve.

Coming to the entrance to the choir, they shall question those
standing about:

> Tell us, People of Jerusalem, where is the hope of
> nations? Where is he, born King of the Jews, whom
> we recognized by signs in the heavens and come to
> adore?

Herod, when he sees this, shall send to them an Armed Man to
sing:

> What discovery or what cause brings you to brave
> unfamiliar roads? What is your destination? Which
> your people? Where your home? Do you come in
> peace, or for war?

The reply of the Magi:

> We are from Chaldea and we come in peace. We
> seek the King of Kings whose birth is proclaimed by a
> star which shines like lightning, brighter than the
> others.

The Armed Man, on his return, shall salute the King on bended
knee, and sing:

> May the King live forever!

Herodes:

> *Salvet te, gratia mea.*

Armiger, ad Regem:

> *Adsunt nobis, Domine, tres viri ignoti ab oriente*
> *venientes, noviter natum quemdam regem queritantes.*

Tunc mittat Herodes Oratores vel Interpretes ad Magos, dicens[1]:

> *Leti Inquisitores, qui sint[2] inquirite reges[3],*
> *Affore, quo[4] nostris iam fama revolvit in oris[5].*

Interpretes ad Magos:

> *Principis edictu, Reges,/ prescrire venimus*
> *Quo sit directus[6] hic[7] vester et unde profectus.*

Magi:

> *Regem quesitum duce stella significatum,*
> *Munere proviso properamus eum venerando.*

Oratores, reversi ad [H]erodem:

> *Reges sunt Arabum. Cum trino munere natum*
> *Querunt infantem quem monstrant sidera regem.*

---

[1] MS: dicentes   [2] MS: sunt
[3] corrected from "regis" in the MS   [4] MS: quos
[5] this word is preceded by two obliterated letters, perhaps "ch"

Herod:

> *And you, in my favour.*

The Armed Man, to the King:

> *To us, Lord, have come three strangers from the East,*
> *seeking a certain new-born king.*

Let Herod then send Spokesmen as his agents to the Magi,
singing:

> *My good Inquisitors, find out who these kings are.*
> *Look to it, for already rumours are being repeated in*
> *our territories.*

The Agents, to the Magi:

> *Kings! By order of His Majesty we come to find out*
> *why you came here, and from where.*

The Magi:

> *The king we seek has been shown to us by a star.*
> *Furnished with a tribute we hasten to pay him homage.*

The Spokesmen, having returned to Herod:

> *They are kings from Arabia. With a threefold gift*
> *they seek a new-born child whom the stars show to be a*
> *king.*

---

[6] MS: profectus. This reading is from Paris, Bibliothèque Nationale, MS lat.
16819 (of the eleventh century, from Compiègne), fol. 49.

[7] inserted between the lines

Herodes, mittens Armigerum pro Magis:

> *Ante venire iube, quo possim singula scire*
> *Qui sint[1], cur veniant, quonam[2] rumore requirant.*

Armiger:

> *Quod mandas, cicius, Rex inclite, proficietur.*

Armiger, ad Magos:

> *Regia vos mandata vocant. Non segniter[3] ite!*

Armiger, adducens Magos ad Herodem:

> *En Magi veniunt,*
> *Et regem natum, stella duce, requirunt.*

Herodes, ad Magos:

> *Que sit causa vie? Qui vos, vel unde venitis? Dicite!*

Magi:

> *Rex est causa vie; reges sumus ex Arabitis*
> *Huc veni/entes.*
> *Querimus en Regem regnantibus imperitantem,*
> *Quem natum mundo lactat Iudaica virgo.*

---

[1] MS: sunt   [2] MS: quo nos   [3] MS: signiter

[56]

Herod, sending the Armed Man for the Magi:

> *Order them to come first to me, that I may know precisely who they are, why they have come, and what news brought this search about.*

The Armed Man:

> *What you command, illustrious King, will be carried out immediately.*

The Armed Man, to the Magi:

> *Royal commands summon you.*
> *Be not slow in obedience.*

The Armed Man, leading the Magi to Herod:

> *Here are the Magi. Guided by a star they have come seeking a new-born king.*

Herod, to the Magi:

> *What is the purpose of your journey? Who are you, and whence do you come? Speak!*

The Magi:

> *A king is the cause of our journey; we ourselves are kings, and we come here from Moorish lands. This king we seek rules over rulers. He is just born, and now nursed by a Jewish maid.*

Herodes, ad Magos:

> *Regem quem queritis, natum esse quo signo[1] didicistis?*

Magi:

> *Illum natum esse didicimus in oriente stella monstrante.*

Herodes:

> *Si illum regnare creditis, dicite nobis!*

Magi:

> *Illum regnare fatentes, cum misticis muneribus de terra longinqua adorare venimus, ternum Deum venerantes tribus cum muneribus.*

Et ostendant munera. Primus dicat:

> *Auro regem.*

Secundus:

> *Thure Deum.*

Tercius:

> *Mirra mortalem.*

Tunc Herodes imperet Simmistis[2], qui cum eo sedent in habitu iuvenili, ut adducant Scribas, qui in diversorio parati sunt barbati:

---

[1] corrected from "sigono" in the MS   [2] MS: simstris

Herod, to the Magi:

> *This king you seek, how did you learn of his birth?*

The Magi:

> *We learned of his birth from a star shining in the East.*

Herod:

> *If you believe in his authority, tell us!*

The Magi:

> *Acknowledging his reign we come with mystic offerings from distant lands to pay tribute to a threefold God with three gifts.*

And they shall show their gifts. Let the first sing:

> *With gold, because a king.*

The second:

> *With incense, because God.*

The third:

> *With myrrh, because a mortal.*

Then Herod shall order the Priests, who, in the dress of young men, sit by him, to bring out the Scribes, who are bearded, and waiting off-stage:

Vos, mei Sim[m]iste, Legis peritos ascite ut discant in prophetis quid senciant ex his.

Sim[m]iste ad Scribas, et adducant eos cum libris prophetarum:

Vos, Legis periti, ad Regem vocati, cum prophetarum libris properando venite!

Postea Herodes int[erro]get Scribas, dicens:/

O vos Scribe interrogati! Dicite si quid de hoc puero scriptum videritis in libro.

Tunc Scribe diu revolvant librum, et tandem, inventa quasi prophecia[1], dicant *Vidimus Domine*, et osten[den]tes cum digito, Regi incredulo tradant librum:

Vidimus, Domine, in prophetarum lineis, nasci Christum[2] in Bethlehem[3] Iude, civitate David, propheta sic vaticinante:

Chorus:

Bethlehem non es minima [in principibus Iuda, ex te enim exiet dux qui regat populum meum Israel; ipse enim salvum faciet populum suum a peccatis eorum.][4]

---

[1] MS: prophecica   [2] MS: christus   [3] MS: Belleem
[4] the MS gives only the cue to this antiphon. It is supplied here from Codex F 160 of Worcester Cathedral (a MS of the thirteenth century), p. 9.

> *You, my Priests, call in men who know the Law to find out what the prophets have to say about this.*

The Priests shall then go and bring forth the Scribes with the books of the prophets:

> *You who know the Law have been summoned to the King. Come quickly, and bring the books of the prophets!*

Thereafter let Herod question the Scribes, singing:

> *You, the Scribes I have called to answer! Say whether you find anything about this boy written in the book.*

The Scribes shall then turn over the pages for a long time. At length, finding what looks like a prophecy, they shall sing *Vidimus Domine*, and pointing with their finger, hand the book to the incredulous King:

> *We read, Lord, in the prophecies, of the birth of the Christ in Bethlehem of Juda, the city of David. The prophet has foretold it thus:*

Chorus:

> *Thou, Bethlehem, art not the least of the tribes of Juda; for out of thee will arise a leader who is to be shepherd of my people Israel; and he will deliver his people of their sins.*

Tunc Herodes, visa prophecia[1], fuore accessus, proiciat librum.
At Filius eius, audito tumultu, procedat pacificaturus patrem,
et stans, salutet eum:

> *Salve, Pater inclite,*
> *Salve, Rex egregie*
> *Qui ubique imperas*
> *[S]ceptra tenens regia.*

Herodes:

> *Fili amantissime,*
> *Digne laudis munere,*
> *Laudis pompam regie*
> *Tuo gerens nomine,*
>
> *Rex est natus forcior*
> *Nobis, et potencior.*
> *Vereor ne solio*
> *Nos extrahet[2] regio.*

Tunc Filius, despective loq[uens] de Christo, offe[rat] se ad
vindictam, dic[ens][3]:

> *Contra illum regulum,*
> *Contra natum parvulum,*
> *Iube, Pater, filium*
> *Hoc inire prelium.*

Tunc demum dimittat Herodes Magos ut inquirant de puero,
et coram eis spondeat Regi nato, dicens/:

---

[1] MS: prophecica   [2] MS: extrabet
[3] some letters at the edge of the page have been obliterated

Herod, when he sees the prophecy, overcome with rage, shall cast the book away. His son, hearing the tumult, shall come to pacify his father, and without kneeling, greet him:

> *God save you, noble Father,*
> *God save you illustrious King,*
> *wielding the royal sceptre you*
> *hold sway the world over.*

Herod:

> *Most loving Son, your*
> *dutiful praise and your*
> *royal name make you*
> *yourself praiseworthy.*
>
> *A king has been born*
> *stronger and more powerful*
> *than we, and I fear he will*
> *overturn our throne.*

Then the Son, speaking contemptuously of Christ, shall offer to wreak vengeance, singing:

> *Against this petty king,*
> *against this new-born child,*
> *command, Father, that your*
> *son begin battle.*

At this point Herod shall send the Magi away to look for the boy, and before them pledge himself to the new-born king, singing:

Ite, et de puero diligenter investigate,
Et invento, redeuntes michi renunciate
Ut et ego veniens adorem eum.

Magis egredientibus, procedat stella eos, que nondum in conspectu Herodis ap[p]areat. Quam ipsi sibi mutuo ostendentes, procedant (Qua visa[1], Herodes et Filius minentur cum gladiis.):

Ecce stella in oriente previsa iterum procedit nos lucida!

Interim Pastores redeuntes a presepe veniant, gaudentes et cantantes in eundo:

O Regem Celi, [cui talia famulantur obsequia! Stabulo ponitur qui continet mundum. Jacet in presepio et in nubibus tonat.][2]

Ad quos Magi:

Quem vidistis?

Pastores:

Secundum quod dictum est ab Angelo de puero isto, invenimus infantem pannis involutum et positum in presepio in medio duum animalium.

Postea, Pastoribus abeuntibus, Magi procedant post stellam usque ad presepe, cantantes:

[1] MS: visat
[2] the MS gives only the cue to this respond. It is supplied here from Codex F 160 of Worcester Cathedral, p. 30.

[64]

> *Go, and diligently search out the boy; and when you*
> *have found him come back and report to me so that I*
> *too may come and worship him.*

As the Magi leave, the star, as yet unnoticed by Herod, shall precede them. Drawing one another's attention to it, let them set out (When Herod and his Son catch sight of the star they are to brandish their swords.):

> *Look! The star we beheld in the East once again sends*
> *its rays before us.*

Meanwhile the Shepherds are to come along on their way back from the manger, singing joyfully as they go:

> *O King of Heaven! Are these the honours due him?*
> *Sheltered in a stable is he who shelters the world.*
> *Lying in a manger is he who thunders in the clouds.*

To them, the Magi:

> *Whom have you seen?*

The Shepherds:

> *Following what the Angel told us about this boy,*
> *we found a child in swaddling clothes lying between*
> *two beasts in a manger.*

After the Shepherds have gone, let the Magi set out after the star to the manger, singing:

Que[m] non prevalent propria magnitudine

Celum, terra atque maria lata capere,

De virgineo natus utero ponitur in presepio.

Sermo cecinit quem vatidicus: sta[n]t simul bos et asinus.|

Sed oritur stella lucida, prebitura[1] Domino obsequia,

Quam[2] Balaam ex Iudaica nascituram[3] dixerat prosapia.

Hec nostrorum occulos fulguranti lumine prestrinxit lucida,

Et nos ipsos provide ducens ad cunabula resplendens fulgida.

Tunc Obstetrices, videntes Magos, alloquantur:

Qui sunt hii qui, stella duce, nos adeuntes inaudita ferunt?

Magi:

Nos sumus, quos cernitis, reges Tharsis et Arabum et Saba dona ferentes Christo nato, Regi, Domino, quem, stella ducente, adorare venimus.

Obstetrices, ostendentes puerum:

Ecce puer adest quem queritis; iam properate et adorate, quia ipse est redempcio mundi.

Magi, [primus][4]:

Salve, Rex Seculorum!

[1]MS: prebitum   [2] MS: quem   [3] MS: nasciturum

[4] the distribution of these utterances is clear in the MS from the use of large initials

He whose vastness the heavens, the earth, and the broad seas cannot encompass has been born from the womb of a maid and lies in a manger. What we have heard fulfills the prophecy: ox and ass stand together. But a bright star is rising, which Balaam said would spring from the Jewish race to serve the Lord. The bright flashing of its rays, blinding to our eyes, lights our way safely to the glorious cradle.

The Midwives, catching sight of the Magi, shall address them:

Who are these men led by the star, who come to us speaking of such strange things?

The Magi:

We whom you see are the kings of Tharsis, Arabia, and Sheba; and guided by a star we have come with gifts to worship the new-born Christ, the Lord and King.

The Midwives, revealing the boy:

Here is the boy whom you seek; now hasten to worship him, for he is the world's redeemer.

The Magi, the first:

Blessed be the King of Ages!

[secundus:]

> *Salve, Deus deorum!*

[Tercius:]

> *Salve, salus/ mortuorum!*

Tunc, procidentes, Magi adorent puerum et offerent. Primus dicat:

> *Suscipe, Rex, aurum, regis signum.*

Secundus[1]:

> *Suscipe thus, Tu[2] vere Deus.*

Tercius:

> *Suscipe mirram, signum sepulture.*

Istis factis, Magi incipiant dormire ibi ante presepe donec Angelus (desuper ap[p]arens) moneat in sompnis ut redeant in regionem suam per aliam[3] viam. Angelus dicat:

> *Impleta sunt omnia que prophetice scripta sunt.*
> *Ite, viam remeantes aliam, nec delatores tanti Regis*
> *puniendi eritis.*

---

[1] in the MS the second Magus sings what is here given to the third, and vice versa
[2] this word is inserted between the lines
[3] in the MS "per aliam" is written twice

The second:

> *Blessed be the God of gods!*

The third:

> *Blessed be the Dead's deliverer!*

Then, falling down, the Magi shall worhip the boy and make their offering. The first shall sing:

> *Accept, King, gold, the royal symbol.*

The second:

> *Accept incense, Thou who art true God.*

The third:

> *Accept myrrh, the sign of burial.*

When they finish the Magi shall fall asleep just in front of the manger. Whereupon the Angel (appearing on high) shall warn them in a dream to return to their own land by a different route. Let the Angel sing:

> *What the prophets have written has been fulfilled.*
> *Go now home by another road, and suffer not as the*
> *betrayers of such a King.*

Magi, evigilantes:

> *Deo gracias! Surgamus ergo, visione moniti angelica,*
> *et calle mutato, lateant Herodem que vidimus de puero.*

Tunc Magi, abeuntes, cantent per aliam viam, non vidente Herode:

> *O admirabile commercium!*
> *Creator generis [humani animatum corpus sumens,*
> *de virgine nasci dignatus est. Et procedens homo sine*
> *semine, largitus est nobis suam deitatem.]*[1]

Tunc venientes in choro dicentes:

> *Gaudete, Fratres,*
> *Christus nobis natus est,*
> *Deus homo factus est.*

Tunc cantor incipit:

> *Te Deum...*

Sic finit.

---

[1] only the cue to this antiphon is given in the MS. It is supplied here from Codex F 160 of Worcester Cathedral, p. 50.

The Magi, waking:

> *Thanks be to God! Let us take the warning of the Angel in the vision and depart, changing our route to keep what we know of the boy from Herod.*

The Magi, having avoided Herod, shall sing as they leave by another way:

> *O wonderful bargain!*
> *Mankind's creator, taking to himself a living body, saw fit to be born of a virgin; and although unbegotten by man, made us heirs of his godhead.*

Then entering the choir singing:

> *Rejoice, Brothers, Christ is born to us; God is made man.*

Then the cantor shall intone:

> *Thou, God…*

And thus it concludes.

DRAMATIS PERSONAE

Angel

Heavenly Hosts (chorus)

Shepherds

Two Midwives

Three Magi

Armed Man

Herod

Herod's Agents

High Priests

Scribes

Herod's Son